Investigate

Sound

Chris Oxlade

Heinemann LIBRARY

www.heinemann.co.uk/library
Visit our website to find out more information about Heinemann Library books.

To order:
☎ Phone 44 (0) 1865 888066

🖹 Send a fax to 44 (0) 1865 314091

💻 Visit the Heinemann Bookshop at www.heinemann.co.uk/library to browse our catalogue and order online.

Heinemann Library is an imprint of Pearson Education Limited, a company incorporated in England and Wales having its registered office at Edinburgh Gate, Harlow, Essex, CM20 2JE – Registered company number: 00872828

Heinemann is a registered trademark of Pearson Education Ltd.
Text © Pearson Education Limited 2008
First published in hardback in 2008
Paperback edition first published in 2009
The moral rights of the proprietor have been asserted.

Edited by Sarah Shannon, Catherine Clarke, and Laura Knowles
Designed by Joanna Hinton-Malivoire, Victoria Bevan, and Hart McLeod
Picture research by Liz Alexander and Rebecca Sodergren
Production by Duncan Gilbert
Originated by Chroma Graphics (Overseas) Pte. Ltd
Printed and bound in China by Leo Paper Group

ISBN 978 0 431932 77 4 (hardback)
12 11 10 09 08
10 9 8 7 6 5 4 3 2 1
ISBN 978 0 431932 96 5 (paperback)
13 12 11 10 09
10 9 8 7 6 5 4 3 2 1

British Library Cataloguing in Publication Data
Oxlade, Chris
  Sound. - (Investigate)
  534
A full catalogue record for this book is available from the British Library.

Acknowledgements
We would like to thank the following for permission to reproduce photographs: ©Alamy pp. **5**, **30** (Juniors Bildarchiv), **8** (Phil Degginger); ©Corbis pp. **19** (Roy McMahon), **23** (Daniel Attia/zefa), **10**, **24**; ©FLPA pp. **17** (Philip Perry), **21** (Frans Lanting), **28** (Michael Durham/Minden Pictures); ©Getty Images pp. **6** (Digital Vision), **7** (Stockbyte), **11** (Dorling Kindersley), **12** (Robert Manella), **15**, **22**, **23**, **26**, **30** (PhotoDisc), **18** (joSon), **25** (Pat LaCroix/Stone); ©Jupiter Images p. **9**; ©Lebrecht Music pp. **14** (C. Christodoulou), **28** (Nigel Luckhurst); ©NHPA p. **27** (S Dalton); ©Photolibrary p. **4** (Reiter Daniel), **16** (Digital Vision); ©Science Photo Library p. **22** (Martyn F. Chillmaid).
Cover photograph of boy playing the trumpet reproduced with permission of ©Corbis (Sean Justice).

Every effort has been made to contact copyright holders of material reproduced in this book. Any omissions will be rectified in subsequent printings if notice is given to the publishers.

Disclaimer
All the Internet addresses (URLs) given in this book were valid at the time of going to press. However, due to the dynamic nature of the Internet, some addresses may have changed, or sites may have changed or ceased to exist since publication. While the author and Publishers regret any inconvenience this may cause readers, no responsibility for any such changes can be accepted by either the author or the Publishers.

Contents

Some words are shown in bold, **like this**. You can find out what they mean by looking in the glossary.

Sound around us

Sound is all around us every day. Listening to different sounds tells us about the world around us.

Listen carefully to the sounds you can hear. Are people speaking to each other? Can you hear traffic outside? Are there birds singing?

 The noise dogs make is called a bark.

Making sound

People, animals, machines, and musical **instruments** are just a few things that make sound. People make sounds by talking, shouting, and singing.

Q How are sounds made?

CLUES
- Think about how you play a drum.
- Feel your throat when you hum.

7

Things that shake make sound. Scientists use the word "vibration" for shaking.

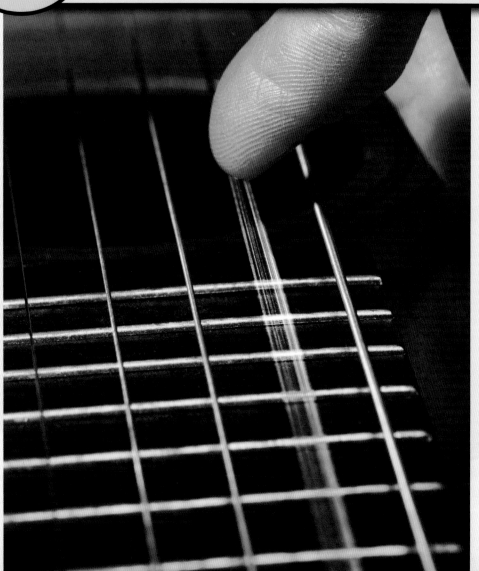

← A guitar string makes a sound. When a guitar string is plucked, it vibrates from side to side. This vibration makes a sound.

You talk, shout, or sing using your throat and mouth. Parts of your throat and mouth **vibrate**. They make the sound of your voice.

Musical sounds

Musical **instruments** make sound. Different instruments make sound in different ways.

How would you make the instruments on these pages make a sound?

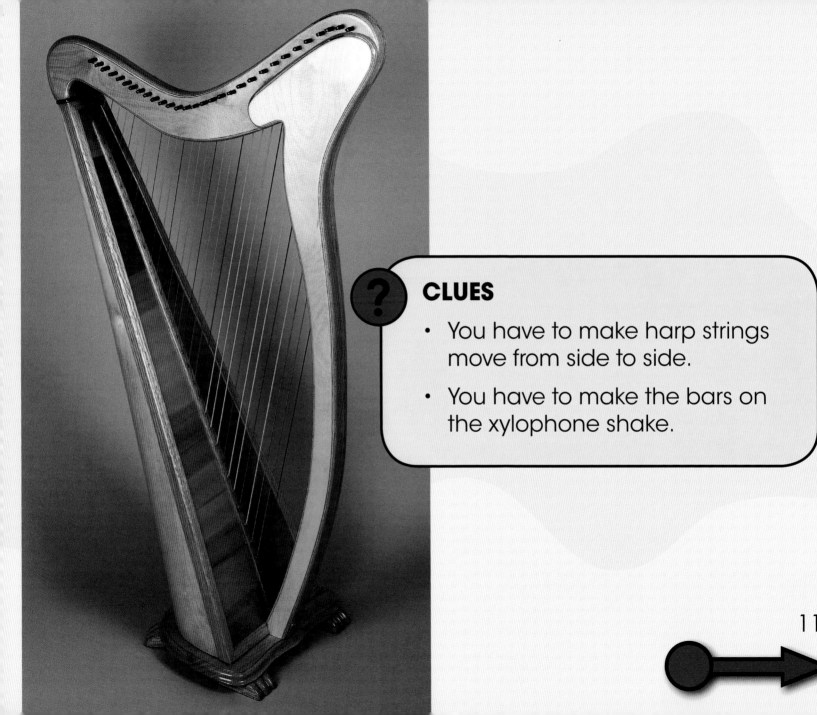

CLUES

- You have to make harp strings move from side to side.

- You have to make the bars on the xylophone shake.

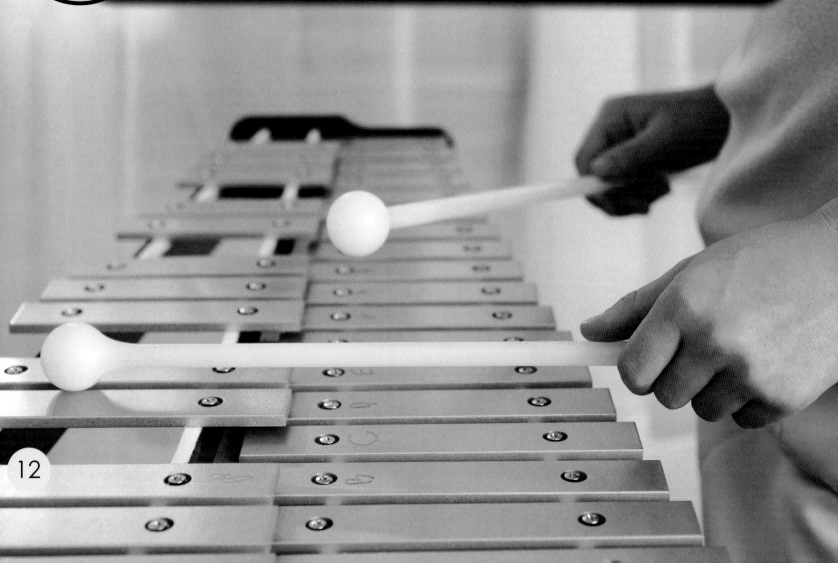

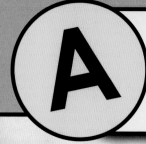

You pluck the strings of a harp to make a sound. You hit a xylophone to make a sound.

We can put different **instruments** into groups.
The instruments in each group make sound in
different ways. Here are two of the groups:

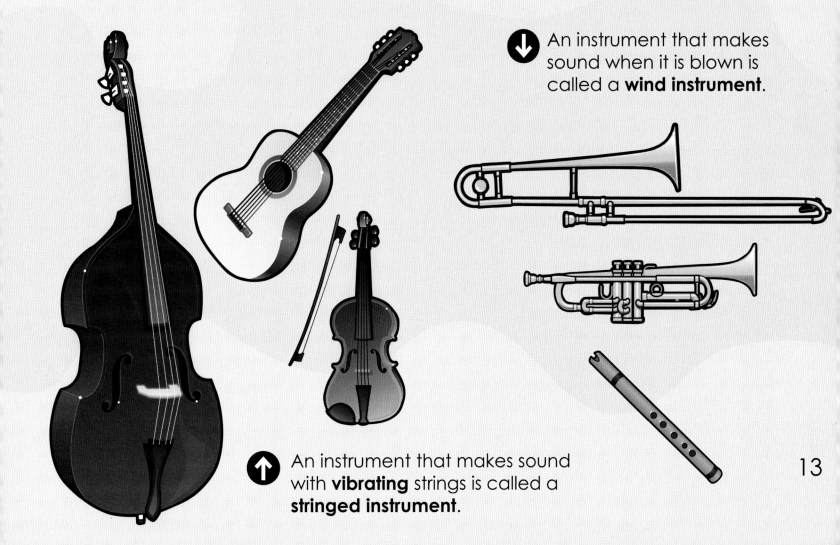

An instrument that makes
sound when it is blown is
called a **wind instrument**.

An instrument that makes sound
with **vibrating** strings is called a
stringed instrument.

Hearing sound

Q Which one of your senses do you use to listen to sound?

?

CLUE

- Try naming your five senses.

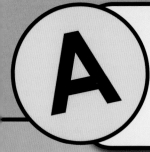
A

You use your sense of hearing to listen to sound. Your ears feel vibrations coming through the air. They send messages to your brain.

Animals hear sound with their ears. Some animals have very good hearing. They can hear very quiet sounds from far away.

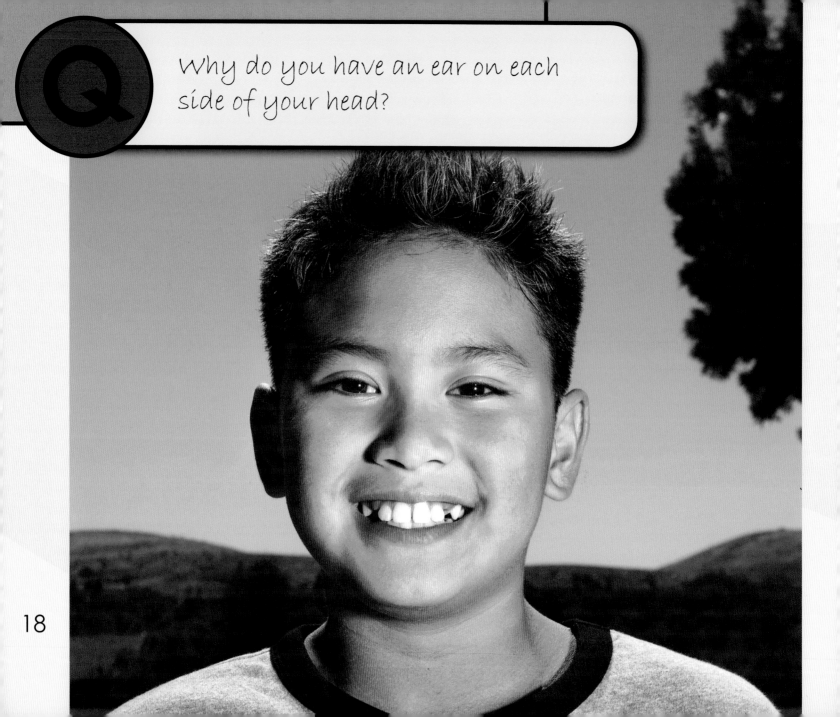

Why do you have an ear on each side of your head?

CLUES

- Turn round and round as you listen to a friend talking.

- Try covering one ear with your hand. Can you tell where sounds are coming from?

- Try covering both ears. Can you still hear the sounds around you?

19

You have two ears so that you can tell where sounds are coming from. A sound coming from one side sounds louder in one ear than the other. This tells your brain where the sound came from.

woof

Many animals need to know where sounds come from. They use their hearing to listen for animals that might be hunting them.

21

Loud and quiet sounds

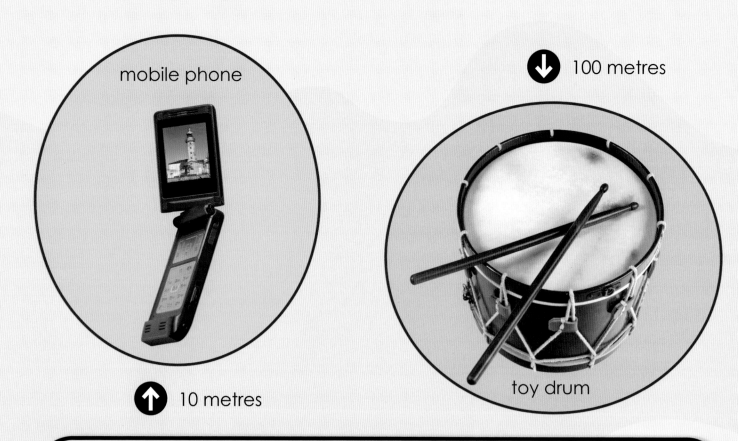

mobile phone

↑ 10 metres

↓ 100 metres

toy drum

In an **experiment** children measured from how far away they could hear different sounds. Here are their results. Which sound was the loudest?

60 metres

stereo

people talking

20 metres

CLUES

- Do you think loud sounds travel further than quiet sounds?

- Can you hear quiet sounds from a long way away?

23

 The toy drum was the loudest sound. Loud sounds always travel further than quiet sounds. This means you can hear loud sounds from further away than quiet sounds.

24

 During a storm, we can hear the rumble of thunder from many kilometres away.

When a sound is made it travels through the air. As it travels, it slowly gets weaker. The further you are from an object that makes a sound, the quieter it seems. This is the same as light from a bulb, which gets dimmer as you move away from the bulb.

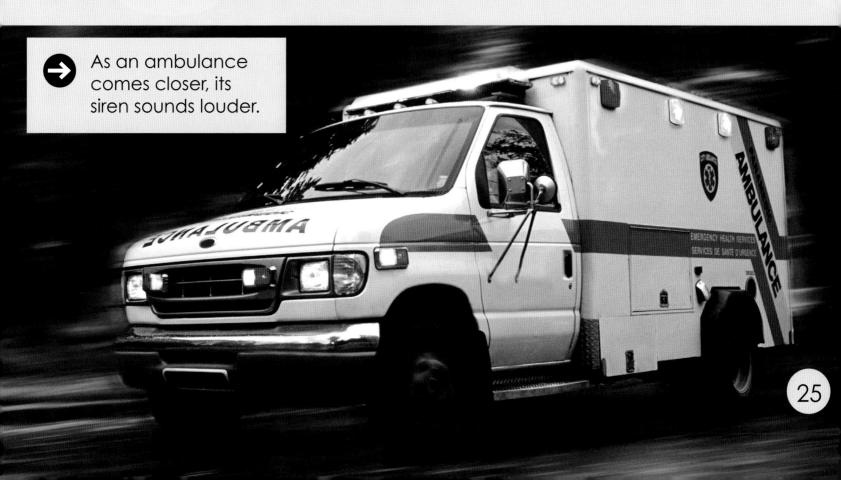

→ As an ambulance comes closer, its siren sounds louder.

Using sound

Sound is a good way of **communicating**. Some machines make a noise to let us know they have finished a job. Others make a sound to warn us of danger.

A smoke alarm makes a loud noise if a fire starts.

Animals make sound to let other animals know they are there, and to warn other animals about danger.

tail

 A rattlesnake rattles its tail to warn other animals not to come near.

Listening to natural sounds and some types of music helps us to relax and feel calm. Other types of music make us feel lively. We also enjoy singing together.

Sound is around us all the time. Things make sound when they **vibrate**. We hear the vibrations with our ears. Sound lets us **communicate**. It warns us. It entertains us. It tells what is happening around us.

29

Checklist

Things that **vibrate** make sounds.

All these things make sounds:

people   animals   machines   musical **instruments**

➡ We hear sounds with our ears.

➡ We have two ears so that we can tell where sounds are coming from.

➡ Loud sounds travel further than quiet sounds.

30

Glossary

communicate send information from one place to another

experiment activity used to test an idea

instrument object that makes musical sounds

stringed instrument musical instrument that makes sound with vibrating strings

vibrate move one way then the other, from side to side, or up and down

wind instrument musical instrument that makes sound when it is blown

Index